Abraham Lincoln and Photographs

If you were living in one of the northern or eastern states during the 1860 election, a painting or a poster wouldn't have caught your eye. Instead, a photograph of Abraham Lincoln might have taken you by surprise. Unlike silly cartoons and scary drawings of Lincoln, this photograph was a real image.

"He looks normal," you might have said. "He will make a good president." But in the South, not even a photograph of Lincoln could convince them.

SURPRISING FACTS

1846–*Artist John Plumbe takes the first photograph of a president inside the White House. But because newspapers were not able to print photographs, few people saw this portrait of James Polk.*

1860–*New Yorker Matthew Brady takes a photograph of Abraham Lincoln. The print is sold in stores throughout the nation. Currier and Ives also copy the image.*

1873–The New York Daily Graphic *becomes the first newspaper to reproduce a photograph.*

Did a Photograph Help Elect Lincoln President?

Cartoons made fun of Abraham Lincoln because he grew up in a log cabin in a western state. Some people thought Lincoln was so backwards that he never changed his socks. Lincoln decided to show everyone he was an ordinary, normal man. Matthew Brady took Lincoln's photograph with a camera. The camera reflected light on a wet, silver-coated plate to capture Lincoln's real image. Sunlight developed the image on paper. Sold in stores, the photograph improved Lincoln's standing. Lincoln said Brady helped him to become president.

Grover Cleveland and Stereographs

If you were living in 1886, chances are you would have enjoyed a popular game. You and your friends would have traded cards showing two pictures that were nearly the same.

When President Grover Cleveland married his young bride, you would have wanted to know what she looked like. To find out, you would have bought a stereograph of the presidential pair. Using your magic glasses, you would have then seen Grover and Frances as one picture in 3-D.

SURPRISING FACTS

1886–President Grover Cleveland becomes the first and only president to marry in a White House ceremony. Photographers sell stereographs or 3-D photo cards of the presidential couple. The Smithsonian's American History Museum owns the originals. The Library of Congress has a large collection of stereographs. Underwood and Underwood of Ottawa, Kansas, was a leader in printing stereographs.

1888–George Eastman sells a portable camera called a Kodak. The American public can now take their own photographs.

1890s–President and Mrs. Cleveland worry about their family's safety when news reporters and crowds of people wait outside the White House to take photographs of their daughters.

1896–Matthew Brady dies. During his lifetime, he photographed 18 presidents.

Where Are My 3-D Glasses?

Your left eye sees images at a different angle than your right eye. In this same way, photographers took two photos of the same image at slightly different angles. Then they printed the photos side by side to make a card called a stereograph. When viewed with a special pair of glasses known as a stereoscope, the two images appeared as one picture. The picture had width, height, and depth–three dimensions or 3-D. Americans in the 1800s traded and collected stereographs like kids today collect sports and movie trading cards.

Theodore Roosevelt and Silent Movies

What if you were alive in 1905, when the movies were silent and the tickets cost a nickel apiece? You might have gone to the movie theater to see what the president looked like. What a treat it would have been to watch President Theodore Roosevelt save Goldilocks and Baby Bear in the latest release.

"Was that really President Roosevelt, or was that an actor?" you might have wondered.

Was Theodore Roosevelt Also a Movie Star?

An actor played President Theodore Roosevelt in a movie called "The 'Teddy' Bear." The film made fun of a popular story about President Roosevelt saving a bear cub. Toy bears were named teddy bears after Roosevelt. Photographers took movies of important events in his life. One film showed Roosevelt as he became the first former president to fly in an airplane. Because adding sound to films came after Roosevelt was president, you can watch – but not hear – many of these films on the Library of Congress' website, www.loc.gov.

Franklin Roosevelt and Movie Newsreels

If you grew up in the 1930s, then you and everyone else would have lived without much money. Times were tough. Hearing and seeing President Franklin Delano Roosevelt in a newsreel at the movies might have given you a lift as you listened and watched his hope-filled talks to the American people.

"Happy days are here again," you might have felt like singing.

How Do Motion Pictures Work?

As film moves through a movie projector, a lamp lights each frame. One picture at a time appears on the screen. The pictures move so fast, your eyes see motion. By the time Theodore Roosevelt's distant cousin, Franklin Roosevelt, became president, movies included sound. Before television, Americans watched the news in newsreels shown between films at a movie theater. Many people saw and heard Franklin Roosevelt's popular radio speeches.

SURPRISING FACTS

1924–*Calvin Coolidge becomes the first president featured in a campaign newsreel at the movies.*

1925–*There are more than 18,000 movie theaters in the United States.*

1927–*Sound arrives at the movies.*

1942–*Franklin Roosevelt's Scottish terrier, Fala, becomes the first presidential pet to star in a movie.*

Kennedy and Nixon and TV Debates

If you were growing up in 1960, you wouldn't have gone to the movies to watch the news. You would have watched television, along with almost everyone else on your block. The event of the year was John F. Kennedy and Richard Nixon's televised debate. You would have seen what two future presidents looked like.

SURPRISING FACTS

1939– *President Franklin Roosevelt becomes the first president to speak on television, but fewer than 200 Americans owned a television set at the time.*

1955– *President Dwight Eisenhower becomes the first to answer questions from reporters for TV. Most Americans now own a TV set.*

1960–*Future Presidents John F. Kennedy and Richard Nixon hold the first campaign debates on TV and radio. They first debate in Chicago.*

1989–*President Ronald Reagan becomes the first president whose entire presidency was covered by CNN, the first 24-hour cable television news network.*

Who Won the Debate, Kennedy or Nixon?

Most Americans owned a television set by 1955. John F. Kennedy and Richard Nixon ran against each other for president in 1960. They held a debate so each could explain why he should be president. Americans who listened by radio thought Nixon won the debate. Those who watched TV thought Kennedy won. Unlike Nixon, Kennedy wore TV makeup and smiled even when he wasn't talking. Americans thought Kennedy looked better on TV, but Nixon sounded better on radio. Kennedy won the election that year, while Nixon won eight years later.

Today's President's Image – Everywhere

If you want to know what the president looks like today, what do you do? Unlike in George Washington's time, today presidential images are everywhere you look – paintings, posters, newspapers, coins, T-shirts, TV, the Internet, and even in this book. Still, if you ever have the chance to meet the president in person, it's something you don't want to ever forget. So...

How Do Web Pages Work?

Your computer is wired to a network of other computers called the Internet. To view a web page, your computer sends a request to a service provider, an organization that owns many computers. The service provider sends your request to the computer holding the web page information. That computer sends your computer the photographs, text, and video of the web page you want to see.

SURPRISING FACTS

1969–The U.S. military connects computers at four locations under a secret plan. In less than four years, this network becomes a large collection of computers called the Internet.

1993–The ability to combine words and pictures on the Internet becomes available to the public. The World Wide Web is born.

1994–President Bill Clinton launches the first White House website, www.whitehouse.gov.

2001–For the first time, whitehouse.gov displays daily videos and photographs of President George W. Bush.

2002–President George W. Bush's dog, Barney, becomes the first presidential pet to appear in a White House web video. Taken from his dog eye-level, Barney's video is a tour of the White House Christmas and holiday decorations.

Barack Obama and Digital Cameras

Be sure to shake the president's hand and take a picture with your digital camera. Thanks to this and other inventions, you now know what Barack Obama – and the other presidents before him – look like.

SURPRISING FACTS

2007–Democratic candidate Hillary Clinton announces her decision to run for president through a video on her website. Republican candidate Fred Thompson announces his decision to run for president through a video on his website.

2008–Candidates from both parties participate in debates with questions posed by people in videos through the Internet on YouTube.

2008–Barack Obama becomes the first African-American to be elected president.

2009–President Barack Obama becomes the first president to carry a smartphone, so he can instantly communicate with his senior staff.

George Washington

John Adams

Thomas Jefferson

James Madison

James Monroe

James K. Polk

Zachary Taylor

Millard Fillmore

Franklin Pierce

James Buchanan

Chester A. Arthur

Grover Cleveland

Benjamin Harrison

Grover Cleveland

William McKinley

Herbert Hoover

Franklin D. Roosevelt

Harry S. Truman

Dwight D. Eisenhower

John F. Kennedy

George H. W. Bush

William J. Clinton

PRESIDENTS

 John Quincy Adams

 Andrew Jackson

 Martin Van Buren

 William Henry Harrison

 John Tyler

 Abraham Lincoln

 Andrew Johnson

 Ulysses S. Grant

 Rutherford B. Hayes

 James Garfield

 Theodore Roosevelt

 William Howard Taft

 Woodrow Wilson

 Warren G. Harding

 Calvin Coolidge

 Lyndon B. Johnson

 Richard M. Nixon

 Gerald R. Ford

 James Carter

 Ronald Reagan

 George W. Bush

 Barack Obama

RESOURCE MATERIALS:

Library of Congress
http://www.loc.gov

National Portrait Gallery
http://www.npg.si.edu

National Gallery of Art
http://www.nga.gov

Newseum
http://www.newseum.org

Smithsonian Institution
http://www.si.edu

U.S. National Archives and Records
http://www.archives.gov

White House
http://www.whitehouse.gov

White House Historical Association
http://www.whitehousehistory.org

PRESIDENTIAL LIBRARIES AND MUSEUMS:

Herbert Hoover
http://hoover.archives.gov

Franklin D. Roosevelt
http://www.fdrlibrary.marist.edu

Harry S. Truman
http://www.trumanlibrary.org

Dwight D. Eisenhower
http://www.eisenhower.archives.gov

John F. Kennedy
http://www.jfklibrary.org

Lyndon B. Johnson
http://www.lbjlibrary.org

Richard M. Nixon
http://www.nixonlibrary.gov

Gerald R. Ford
http://www.fordlibrarymuseum.gov

Jimmy Carter
http://www.jimmycarterlibrary.gov

Ronald Reagan
http://www.reagan.utexas.edu

George H.W. Bush
http://bushlibrary.tamu.edu

William J. Clinton
http://www.clintonlibrary.gov

George W. Bush
http://georgewbushlibrary.gov

ABOUT THE AUTHOR

Jane Hampton Cook enjoys
making history come to life today
through her books, columns,
speeches, and TV appearances.
A former webmaster for President
George W. Bush, Jane served
in the White House and Texas
governor's office. She is a
frequent guest on the Fox News
Channel and lives with her
husband and two sons in Vienna,
Virginia. www.janecook.com

ABOUT THE ILLUSTRATOR

Adam Ziskie is a Detroit native. He attended Montserrat College of Art, where he majored in Illustration. Adam currently lives in San Francisco, where he is perpetually surrounded by fog.